Santa

THE WHOLE STORY

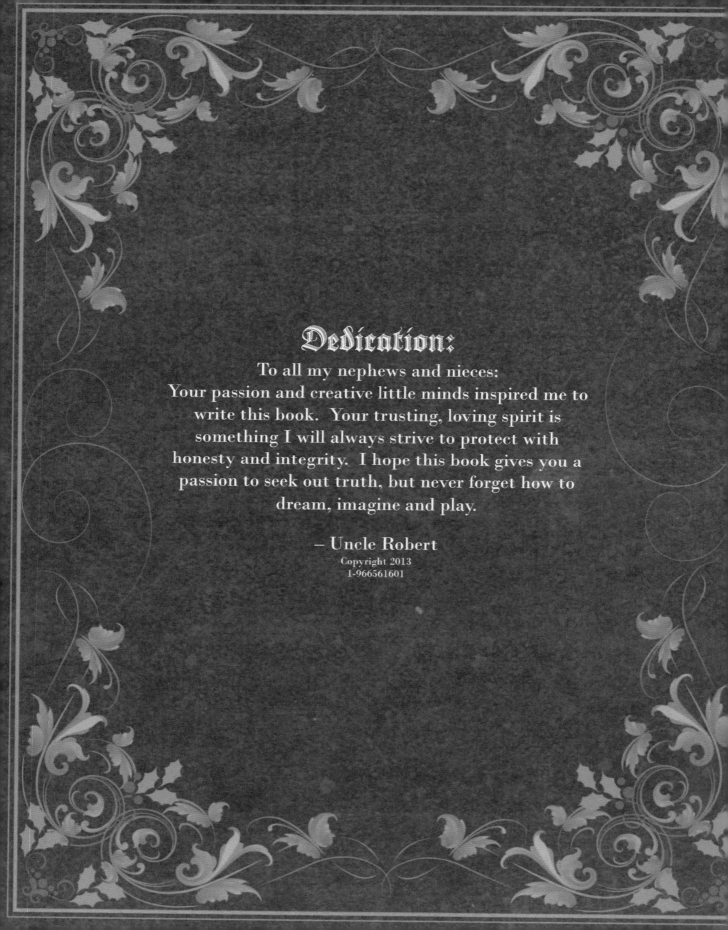

Dedication:

To all my nephews and nieces:
Your passion and creative little minds inspired me to
write this book. Your trusting, loving spirit is
something I will always strive to protect with
honesty and integrity. I hope this book gives you a
passion to seek out truth, but never forget how to
dream, imagine and play.

– Uncle Robert

Table of Contents

THIS IS AN OFFICIAL
PUBLICATION OF

Written by
Robert Weston Gilliard
Copyright 2013
ISBN-13: 978-0615860978 (Robert Weston Gilliard)
ISBN-10: 0615860974

It is a special privilege to receive this book. If you are reading this now, it is because someone thought you were old enough to—not only know the whole truth about Christmas—but bear the responsibility to protect its secrets and truths for generations to come. Are you ready? Do you want to be a member of Santa's Secret Society? Can you help us preserve the magic of Christmas? If so, let's begin...

Is Santa Real?

You might have heard someone say that Santa is not real, but those people just do not know the whole story. The answer is Yes! Santa <u>was</u> a very real man that lived a long time ago, but his memory and spirit is still very much with us today.

He was known by the name Sanctus Nicolaus. There are many variations of his name that are used now that he has become known around the world: Saint Nicolaus, Saint Nick , Santa Claus, Santa, etc.) But for the rest of this book, we will refer to him as Saint Nick!

He was born in 270AD in (what is now) Demre, Turkey...all the way across the sea. When he became a man, he inherited his family's fortune, but spent his life giving that money to the poor and those who needed it more than he. From an early age, Saint Nick was very involved in his church. That is how he came to be known as "saint." Matter-of-fact, you may find him in one of your history books as one of the saints that signed the Nicene Creed.

Santa
AND CHRISTMAS

Saint Nick was known to have loved and defended the traditional story of Jesus birth—which is now celebrated at Christmas. There are some writings that talk about an argument between Saint Nick and a man name Arias. Arias wanted to change some of the details about Jesus birth and Saint Nick would not allow that. While no one knows for sure the whole story of that argument, it is very fitting that Saint Nick would

be forever tied with the Christmas Season, since he cared about that story so much.

YULE-TIDE FEAST – To commemorate Saint Nick and his giving spirit, a week long feast was held on December 6. Originally, the church would secretly deliver grain to the door steps of the poor during this time. As you can see, Saint Nick inspired many people to give and help those in need. That is how his memory is relived every year as we also give to the poor and one another.

CHRISTMAS TODAY: Since then, the calendar has changed and the world celebrates Yule-tide from December 25 to January 1. The birth of Jesus is celebrated on December 25 as well; probably because the story was so near and dear to the heart of Saint Nick.

THE
Christmas
STORY

THE Christmas

STORY AS SAINT NICK WANTED IT PRESERVED

"And there were in the same country shepherds abiding in the field, keeping watch over their flock by night. And, lo, the angel of the Lord came upon them, and the glory of the Lord shone round about them: and they were sore afraid. And the angel said unto them, Fear not; for, behold, I bring you tidings of great joy, which shall be to all people. For unto you is born this day in the city of David a Savior, which is Christ the Lord. And this shall be a sign unto you: Ye shall find the babe wrapped in swaddling clothes, lying in a manger. And suddenly there was with the angel a multitude of the heavenly host praising God, and saying, Glory to God in the highest, and on earth peace and goodwill towards men." All this took place to fulfill what the Lord had said through the prophet: "The virgin will conceive and give birth to a son, and they will call him Immanuel" (which means "God with us").

Luke 2:8-14 and Matthew 1:22-23

Santa:
A LIFE OF GIVING

Santa:
A LIFE OF GIVING

While some of what you may have heard about Saint Nick is myth, you should know that many of those things came from what we know about his life and the way he lived it.   Here is a collection of short stories that are told about his giving nature.

Santa's Bag of Gifts

Much of the story of Saint Nick can be traced back to specific stories of his giving nature. One example is the story of three young girls who were about to be sold into slavery; because their family was very poor. The story is told that Saint Nick gave each girl a bag of coins. The coins were enough to save them from their evil slave-traders. That is probably why we depict Santa today carrying a bag full of good things.

Why We Hang Stockings

Another fun fact about Saint Nick is that he loved to surprise people! It was widely known that if someone left their shoes out, he might drop a few coins in them as he walked by. That is very likely how we got our tradition of putting out Christmas stockings today.

A Christmas Feast

Another story that shapes our Christmas tradition is one called the "Wheat Multiplication." There was a great famine in 311- 312AD in the town of Myra. At that time, Saint Nick convinced a captain of one of King Constantine's ships to unload some wheat to give his village food during the hard times. It really took some convincing for the sea men to take from the king's shipment, but they did. Miraculously, enough wheat was left to feed the village for a year! Yet somehow, even though all that wheat was missing from the ship, their shipment did not change in size or weight and the king was pleased!

This is a great example of how Saint Nick not only practiced a life of giving, but inspired others to give as well. No doubt that town feasted like we do around our Christmas dinner tables.

PROTECTING THE MAGIC OF
Christmas

Yes, Saint Nick was real. History books tell of his accomplishments and life. His good deeds are recorded in history and still live on today through us. Of course, as the world began celebrating Christmas, people began adding little things here and there to the story of Saint Nick. It is all in good fun, and it really does give the holidays a sense of excitement. This is what people refer to as the "Magic of Christmas." It really is a magical time isn't it? And now YOU are part of the magic of keeping this story alive!

You have been entrusted with a legacy that is over 1700 years old. The true story of a Saint that lived defending the true story of Christmas and gave us an example of how we can spread the joy of Christmas.

Certificate

OFFICIAL ACCEPTANCE

I, (your name) _____,
being of age and sound mind—now knowing the
story of Saint Nick—will continue his legacy of
giving and kindness. I hereby will protect this
secret so children younger than I can enjoy the
magic of Christmas as I have. By doing so, I will be
accepted into Santa's Secret Society.

_____

(Your Signature)

Robert W. Gilliard

Robert Weston Gilliard
Founder of Santa's Secret Society
www.santassecretsociety.com

Made in the USA
Coppell, TX
14 November 2024

40265469R00017

Feeling JEALOUS!

First published in 2017 by Wayland

Text copyright © Wayland 2017
Illustrations copyright © Mike Gordon 2017

Wayland
Carmelite House
50 Victoria Embankment
London EC4Y 0DZ

Wayland Australia
Level 17/207 Kent Street
Sydney, NSW 2000

Managing editor: Victoria Brooker
Creative design: Paul Cherrill

ISBN: 978 1 5263 0075 1

Printed in China

MIX
Paper from
responsible sources
FSC
www.fsc.org
FSC® C104740

Wayland is a division of
Hachette Children's Books,
an Hachette UK company.
www.hachette.co.uk

Feeling JEALOUS!

Written by
Kay Barnham

Illustrated by
Mike Gordon

WAYLAND

"It's NOT fair," said Martha, punching a pillow. "What's not fair?" Lucy asked gently. She was Martha's best friend, but even she was a little scared of how cross Martha looked right now.

4

"Samuel goes to bed at eight o'clock,"
huffed Martha, hurling a cuddly hippo
across the bedroom, "and I have
to go at seven. See? *Not fair.*"
"Ah," said Lucy. She did see.

"Mum says I'm silly to feel jealous," added Martha.
"She says that Samuel's older than me,
so of course he should go to bed later."

Lucy thought for a moment.
Then she smiled. If Martha could think of
something good about being the younger one,
then she might feel happier.

"Doesn't Samuel have to unload the dishwasher?" said Lucy.

"Yes," said Martha, looking puzzled.

"And does he put the rubbish out too?" Lucy went on.

"Er, yes," said Martha, beginning to smile. "Mum says he has to do more jobs because he's older..."

Lucy grinned. "Actually," said Martha with a giggle, "I don't like going to bed earlier than Samuel, but I'm not at all jealous about his extra jobs."

At school the next day, George was showing off about his new hoverboard. "It's the best thing ever," he told anyone who would listen. "It's just like flying!"

"I wish he'd shut up about the stupid hoverboard," Katie muttered to Lucy.

"I want one really badly, but my mum says they're too expensive. It's not fair!"

Lucy wondered how she could make Katie look on the bright side. "Maybe you've got a toy that George doesn't have?" she suggested.

"I've got a skateboard," Katie said,
kicking a stone. "It's a bit like a hoverboard.
I suppose I could play with that instead ..."

"... while you're saving up,"
finished Lucy, with a wink.

A smile tugged at the corner of Katie's
mouth. It grew bigger and brighter
and Lucy couldn't help smiling back.

"I could, couldn't I?"
Katie said.

"It would take a long,
long time, but I could
save up and buy my
own hoverboard!"

15

After school, Lucy and her brother Alex went
to visit their Auntie Linda, who had just adopted
a scruffy old terrier called Bob.

"Bob is unbelievably cool," sighed Alex,
rubbing the dog behind the ears.
He loved animals so much.
He wanted to be a vet
when he grew up.

Lucy held her breath.
She knew exactly what
was coming next ...

17

"I want a dog," said Alex. "Or a cat.
Or a hamster. I'd even settle for a gerbil.
I'd look after it really well. Why won't Mum
and Dad let us have one?" he moaned.

"Erm ... because Dad's allergic?" Lucy said quietly.
Dad sneezed if he even looked at a furry animal.
Alex knew this, of course. But it didn't stop him
being jealous of everyone who had a pet.

"Auntie Linda," said Lucy, stroking the little dog, "do you think we might be able to take Bob for walks?"

"Could we sort of *share* him?"

"What a wonderful idea!" said Auntie Linda.
"Why don't we start now?"

And she handed the lead to Alex,
who beamed with happiness.

The following week, it was the school sports' day. Lucy was so excited. She would win every race for her team! Her friends' cheers would be DEAFENING!

Even better, her parents were coming to watch Lucy and her brother take part.

They would be so proud!

But Lucy dropped her egg 27 times in the egg-and-spoon race.

In the sack race, she fell on her face.

In the hurdles race, there wasn't a single hurdle standing when she finished ... in last place.

"Look, Alex is in the hurdles race,"
Martha said to Lucy. "That'll cheer you up.
Your brother's *so* fast."

Alex *was* fast. He was so fast that he finished in first place. Then he won the 100-metre race too.

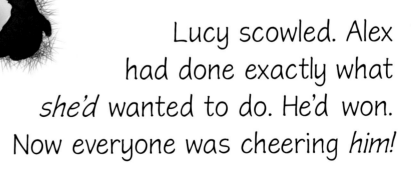

Lucy scowled. Alex had done exactly what *she'd* wanted to do. He'd won. Now everyone was cheering *him!*

"Cheer up, Lucy," Martha said. "I know losing is hard, but the good thing is that your brother did so well."

Lucy saw Alex's shining face.
"I'll try to feel happy for him," she said.

"Besides, Alex is in the athletics team,"
Martha went on. "Why don't you take up a sport?
Then we could be cheering you next year."
Lucy thought for a moment.
She did love swimming ...

"Go on, have one of my medals," said Alex, hanging a medal around Lucy's neck. Lucy smiled at how everyone had bounced her own advice back at her.

And perhaps it was good advice, because now she didn't feel jealous at all.

FURTHER INFORMATION

THINGS TO DO

1. Green is a colour that is often linked with jealousy and envy.
And so jealousy is sometimes known as the green-eyed monster...
Can you draw or paint a picture of your own green-eyed monster?
Make sure it looks super jealous!

2. This book shows lots of things that people might be jealous about,
such as older brothers and sisters, toys, pets and success.
What other things can you think of?

3. Make a colourful word cloud! Start with 'jealous', then add any
other words this makes you think of. Write them all down using
different coloured pens. More important words
should be bigger, less important words smaller.
Start like this...

I WANT THAT!

Jealous envy

NOTES FOR PARENTS AND TEACHERS

The aim of this book is to help children think about their feelings in an enjoyable, interactive way. Encourage them to have fun pointing to the illustrations, making sounds and acting, too. Here are more specific ideas for getting more out of the book:

1. Encourage children to talk about their own feelings, if they feel comfortable doing so, either while you are reading the book or afterwards. Here are some conversation prompts to try:

What makes you feel jealous?
How do you stop feeling jealous when this happens?

2. Make a facemask that shows a jealous expression.

3. Put on a feelings play! Ask groups of children to act out the different scenarios in the book. The children could use their facemasks to show when they are jealous in the play.

4. Hold a jealous-face competition. Who can look the MOST jealous?! Strictly no laughing allowed!

BOOKS TO SHARE

A Book of Feelings by Amanda McCardie,
illustrated by Salvatore Rubbino
(Walker, 2016)

Dinosaurs Have Feelings, Too: Jamal Jealousaurus
by Brian Moses, illustrated by Mike Gordon
(Wayland, 2015)

I Feel Jealous by Brian Moses, illustrated by Mike Gordon
(Wayland, 1994)

Not Fair, Won't Share by Sue Graves,
illustrated by Desideria Guicciardini
(Franklin Watts, 2014)

The Great Big Book of Feelings
by Mary Hoffman, illustrated by Ros Asquith
(Frances Lincoln, 2016)

The Lion, the Witch and the Wardrobe by C S Lewis
(HarperCollins Children's Books, 2009)

READ ALL THE BOOKS
IN THIS SERIES:

Feeling Angry!
ISBN: 978 1 5263 0015 7

Feeling Frightened!
ISBN: 978 1 5263 0077 5

Feeling Jealous!
ISBN: 978 1 5263 0075 1

Feeling Sad!
ISBN: 978 1 5263 0071 3

Feeling Shy!
ISBN: 978 1 5263 0079 9

Feeling Worried!
ISBN: 978 1 5263 0073 7

Journey through

LUXEMBOURG

Photos by
Tina and Horst Herzig

Text by
Sylvia Gehlert

Stürtz

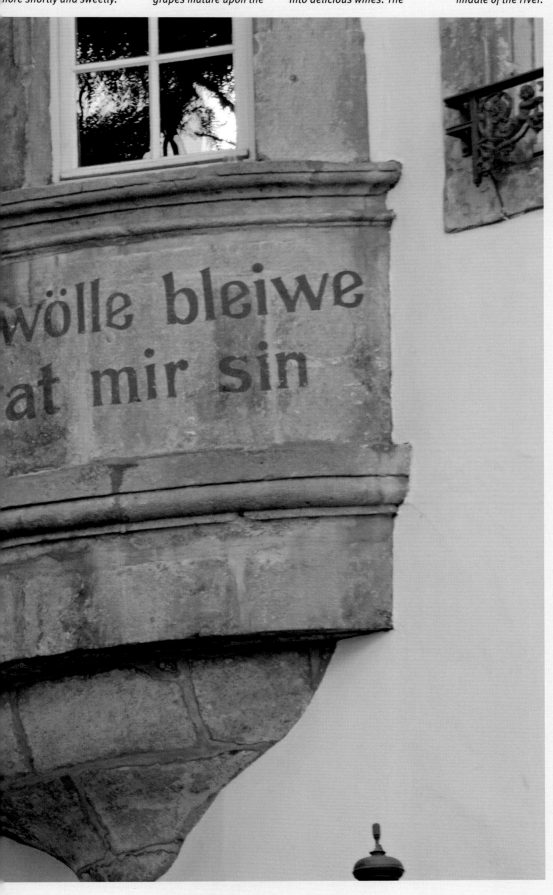

we are." Their unbending will for stability and independence in spite of long centuries of foreign domination couldn't be put more shortly and sweetly.

Pages 10/11: The Moselle by Wormeldange. While it laps leisurely at the shore, grapes mature upon the slopes on both the Luxembourg and German sides, which the traditional winemaking arts transform into delicious wines. The border between the two countries, which share its surveillance and administration, runs down the middle of the river.

Contents

Luxembourg – a jewel set in green

In the year 963, Count Siegfried I of the Ardennes acquired the Bock Fiels from the Trier abbey of Saint Maximin with the remains of a Roman fort called "Lucilinburhuc" in the document. Siegfried began constructing a fortress and the name of the castle soon was lent to the entire dominion of his progeny, the counts of Luxembourg.

Financial stronghold, EU control centre and media giant: these clichés are like those trees that you can't see the forest for. That forest thrives between the Ardennes and the Moselle in lovely diversity, and is quite definitely real. Luxembourg is far more than its cosmopolitan capital city, and even it cannot be reduced to a handy denominator. Luxembourg and its people are unique: cosmopolitan as well as homebodies, hospitable with a sense for the small (great!) joys of life, companionable but not backslapping, imaginative yet pragmatic, patriotic with a scintillating native wit and a feeling for delicate nuances. They are exemplary in many a field, conciliatory yet never preachy, mediators between cultures because of a long, turbulent history that shaped the country and people into something that is beneficial to all of our futures: interest in others, the need to share and understand, the desire to transcend the boundaries in people's minds. This is the contribution made by Luxembourg and its people, unobtrusive and purposeful, from which its neighbours in Europe should learn.

Notwithstanding the astonishing natural beauty and the historic monuments from a good two-thousand years, the wealth of sporting and recreational opportunities, the cultural events and festivities year round, what makes a visit so worthwhile is the reception the country gives its guests: generous, cordial and with no fuss. Your questions are given friendly answers here, you are addressed personally, and with a smile; sourpusses are rarely found.

The inhabitants of the world's only Grand Duchy are proud of their nation and their identity, which they have managed to preserve in spite of all historic upheavals. They stick to their motto: *Mir wëlle bleiwe wat mir sin* (We

12

wish to remain what we are). Conservative, you may say, or even petty? By no means, counter the Luxembourgers: If you wish to remain as you are, you must be prepared for constant change. Talk about dialectics!

As for the natural treasures of this "largest of the small countries of Europe," as its admirers call it, with an area of 2,586 square kilometres (999 square miles) Luxembourg stretches between the German *Lands* of Saarland and Rhineland-Palatinate, the French region of Lorraine and Belgium's French-speaking region of Wallonia. This places the Grand Duchy in the centre of a "greater region" counting over eleven million inhabitants of the alliance of the five bordering regions, in which cross-border initiatives and projects are emphasized. The border to France is 73 kilometres (45 miles) long, to Belgium it is 148 kilometres (92 miles), and to Germany 138 kilometres (86 miles), of which 42 (26 miles) run along the Moselle in the southeast. The three border triangles where Luxembourg meets with two of its neighbours are unique: Germany and France in the southeast, France and Belgium in the southwest, Belgium and Germany in the northeast.

Geographically, Luxembourg differentiates the "Oesling," in the northern half of the country, from the southern "Gutland." The Oesling, of which 358 square kilometres (138 square miles) belong to Germano-Luxembourg Nature Park, forms part of the Ardennes. In this sparsely populated hill country, forested ranges of oaks, common beeches, spruces and maples alternate with deeply incised river valleys. Red deer and wild boars cavort, birds of prey possess ample hunting grounds and the waterways attract anglers. The Sauer, flowing from west to east, is delightful and varied over its approximately 60 kilometres (37 miles) from its source in the Ardennes until it flows into the Moselle. Its upper reaches are dammed to form a 15 kilometre (9 mile) long, winding lake (part of it drinking water reservoir and the rest a paradise for water sport enthusiasts). In its middle section, the river's meandering has dug it deep into the rocky landscape, and the wildly romantic sandstone formations of "Little Switzerland" accompany its lower reaches, until, in a quiet valley, it flows into the *Mosella*, the little Meuse, as the Romans dubbed the Moselle.

The gently rolling "Gutland" in the southern half of the country is primarily used by agriculture; motley cattle on the pastures, orchard meadows, grapes ripening on the Moselle slopes. The "Red Land" in the southwest owes its nickname to its underground treasures: rich

Once a tranquil village, in the 1960s Kirchberg became the centre of a construction boom. In addition to buildings for the European Community, blocks of flats, banks, shopping centres and the Luxembourg trade fair went up. The Catalonian architect Ricardo Bofill designed the triangular Place de l'Europe. In its centre, the expressive lines of the new philharmonic concert hall by Christian de Portzamparc of France are sweeping and dynamic.

deposits of iron ore, which turned the fortunes of the famine-plagued population when industrial exploitation began in the mid-19th century. The struggle to survive had already driven thousands of Luxembourgers to emigrate. Mines and steelworks shot up, the smokestacks spewed and soon Luxembourg's heavy industry provided the foundation for investments elsewhere. The country became economically appealing and has remained so until today, always at pains to find the balance between change and continuity. The mines have now been closed down, the ore for steel production is imported via the Moselle cargo port of Mertert and the domestic steel corporation Arcelor (the world's second largest) merged in 2006 with India's Mittal, the sector's number one. The headquarters of Arcelor-Mittal are located in Luxembourg.

Luxembourg – a mighty fortress
The event-filled history of this small country is due, not least, to its strategically significant location and to the rivalries and appetite for conquest of its larger neighbours. The mechanism is familiar; many a frontier region in Europe suffered a similar fate.
In today's border triangle to France and Belgium is the Luxembourg town of Pétange. There, on the Titelberg, 130 metres (427 feet) above the Chiers valley, the Celtic Trevori erected a mighty, fortified settlement. The discoveries of scores of Gallic coins with approximately thirty different imprints reveal lively trading activities with other Celtic tribes from near and far. When Caesar's legions conquered Gaul, this swathe of land reaching to the Rhenish Limes came under Roman dominion. Shortly before the Common Era, the city "Augusta Treverorum" (modern Trier) was founded on the orders of Caesar Augustus within the tribal

territory of the Trevori, only 80 kilometres (50 miles) from the Titelberg, which would grow to become a significant economic and cultural centre.

The migration of the peoples and the fall of the Empire were the end of the "pax romana," or "Roman peace." For the territory that would later be Luxembourg, this meant conquest by the Germanic Franks and, a few centuries later, becoming part of the empire of Charlemagne. After the partition among Charlemagne's grandsons laid down in the Treaty of Verdun and the shifts in possession that ensued, in 925 Luxembourg became part of the Kingdom of the East Franks, from which the Holy Roman Empire would later emerge.

The story continues like this: In the year 963, the Count of Ardennes Siegfried I undertakes a barter transaction with Trier's abbey of Saint Maximin. He trades some of his lands for a small rock called the Bock Fiels situated above the Alzette Valley, home to the remains of a Roman fort, called "Lucilinburhuc" in the trade document. The castle on the rocks means nothing to the monks, but a great deal to Siegfried, the strategist, for from here, the trading routes that run from Reims to Trier and Cologne can be ideally monitored. This confers political weight upon the lord of the castle and great distinction upon the young noble house of the Counts of Luxembourg, as they call themselves from 1060. From this castle on the Bock Fiels, the name of Luxembourg is transferred to their entire dominion. The castle is expanded to become a fortress, trade and commerce begin to settle here, and a town arises around the rock and on the shores of the Pétrusse and Alzette. In 1354, the county is elevated to a duchy. In the ensuing ages, the house of Luxembourg provides three emperors and a king before its male line expires and the last Duchess offers her country for sale in 1441. The Duchy of Burgundy, powerful rival to the French throne, leaps to make the transaction. Luxembourg is situated on the way to its blossoming possession in the Netherlands, and it wants this pathway secured. But, in 1477, Duke Charles the Bold falls on the battlefield of Nancy and with him, Burgundy falls. The marriage of Charles's daughter to the Habsburg prince and later Emperor Maximilian puts Luxembourg yet again into other hands. And so it goes, over the centuries and from crown to crown. Even the French Revolution changes nothing. On the contrary! Revolutionary troops conquer Luxembourg, which is then incorporated in the First French Republic as the *departement* of "*Forêts*." Following Napoleon's final defeat, the victorious powers debate the fate of Luxembourg at

the Congress of Vienna in 1815. It is named a sovereign Grand Duchy, however governed by the king of the Netherlands in personal union. In addition, it is integrated in the German Confederation, and a Prussian garrison is foisted upon its capital to make it a confederate fortress. When the neighbouring Belgians finally free themselves from Dutch rule in 1839 and establish a kingdom of their own, the Luxembourgers observe the results with mixed feelings. While they do not begrudge the Belgians their hard-won autonomy, nearly half of their own territory – the French-speaking Wallonian west – is lost to the young monarchy through a referendum. As if that weren't enough, in 1867 the French Emperor Napoleon III attempts to buy Luxembourg from the Dutch. The great European powers get jumpy, the "Luxembourg Crisis," ensues and is finally defused by the Second Treaty of London, which declares the Grand Duchy "eternally neutral." The Prussian garrison pulls out and the mighty fortress on the Bock Fiels, the "Gibraltar of the north," is razed. Finally, the Grand Duchy becomes completely independent in 1890. After the death of King William III, his daughter ascends to the Dutch throne. This puts an end to the personal union as the Luxembourgers can appeal to their purely male law of succession and thus elect Adolphe of Nassau-Weilburg, who hails from a sideline of the Dutch dynasty and who lost his German duchy to Prussia, as their head of state. Adolphe's son and heir William IV dies after a brief time on the throne and leaves behind six daughters, but no son and heir. Quickly, the Luxembourgers amend their law: from now on, if there is no male heir a princess may also take over the reign. Marie-Adélaïde, William IV's oldest daughter and a rather mystically oriented young woman, is the first to ascend the throne but abdicates after an unhappy twelve-year reign.

Cradle of modern Europe

Ignoring Luxembourg's neutrality, German troops occupy the country during the First World War. In a referendum in 1919, the people are asked to decide whether the Grand Duchy should continue on as such or become a republic. More than three-fourths vote to retain the monarchy with Marie-Adélaïde's sister Charlotte as head of government. That same year, women are given the right to vote in Luxembourg – decades before many other women in Europe.

The Second World War follows and in May 1940, the country is again occupied by German armed forces. While head of state Charlotte forms an exile government with her ministers in Great Britain and supports the resistance, the Grand Duchy is placed under a *gauleiter* for "integration" into the Third Reich and experiences the whole extent of Nazi suppression and persecution. Liberated by the US army on 10 September 1944, the following winter sees Luxembourg and Belgium become the tragic scene of the Battle of the Bulge.

In June 1945, Luxembourg becomes a member of the United Nations; in 1949, it is a founding member of NATO. Less than five years after the end of the war, Robert Schuman, a native of Luxembourg and French foreign minister, advocates rapprochement between Germany and France as the foundation of a unified Europe of the future. He presents the blueprint for a western European Coal and Steel Community. The plan is named after him, although Jean Monnet, head of the General Planning Commission, is also a principle architect. In Paris on 18 April 1951, the foreign ministers of France, Belgium, Luxembourg, Italy, the Netherlands and West Germany sign the treaty establishing the European Coal and Steel Community, a predecessor of the European Community and today's EU.

Robert Schuman's personal history made him a dedicated advocate of a unified Europe. His mother from Luxembourg and father from Lorraine, Schuman is born in 1886 in the Clausen quarter of Luxembourg City. Although his father was born French, the 1871 annexation of Alsace-Lorraine makes him a German citizen – and hence his wife and child, too. After completing his schooling in Metz, Schuman studies law in Bonn, Munich, Berlin and Strasbourg and opens a law office in Metz. A German reservist in the First World War, he becomes a French citizen after the return of Alsace-Lorraine to France, and a member of the National Assembly until 1940, when he is arrested by the Gestapo. In 1942, he flees to France after escaping imprisonment in Germany and joins

the resistance movement. Between 1946 and 1953, he is consecutively Minister of Finance, Prime Minister and Foreign Minister of France, and then in 1955-56 Minister of Justice. In March 1958, Robert Schuman is unanimously elected the first President of the European Parliament in Strasbourg; the university in that city, where he completed his doctorate, now bears his name.

Land of many languages

For the majority of Luxembourgers, "Lëtzebuergesch" or Luxembourgish, a melodic Moselle Franconian dialect very similar to those spoken in neighbouring parts of Belgium, France and Germany, is their mother tongue and the expression of their identity. It was declared the national language of the Grand Duchy in 1984 and is the country's third official language after French and German. Although similar to German, Luxembourgish can be difficult for native speakers of German to understand. Unlike other Moselle Franconian dialects, the language is greatly influenced by French, borrowing and modifying many French words, such as *Buschauffeur* (bus driver), rather than French *chauffeur de bus*. Some words are entirely different from German and French, like the word for potato, which is *Gromper* in Luxembourgish, but *pomme de terre* in French and *Kartoffel* in High German.

The literature of the nation is written in all three languages and every genre. It is largely unknown outside Luxembourg, but experienced a renaissance in the 1970s and 1980s, when modern-themed novels began to be written in Luxembourgish without any folkloristic tinges. Luxembourgish is used at home and in public life, in parliamentary debates and addresses by His Royal Highness. It is the language taught in preschool and progressively replaced by

High German in primary school. From the second grade, the pupils also learn French. Those who move on to the *Gymnasium* after six years are taught in French and additionally learn English or Latin. German remains the teaching language in other school forms and vocational schools. Luxembourg invests considerably in its language education. The positive effects are obvious. A tiny internal market stands alongside a larger external market alone with the German and French-speaking countries, and for them, young Luxembourgers are linguistically prepared when they enter professional life or venture to study in one of the neighbouring countries. Nearly every sixth Luxembourger is of Portuguese descent, many Italians also settled in the Grand Duchy, in addition to persons of other nationalities, including non-Europeans. All of them preserve their linguistic and cultural traditions and are welcome mediators in the dialogues of the countries of their origin whether near or far.

Luxembourg in figures

The Grand Duchy of Luxembourg is not the airy backdrop of an operetta; rather, under its constitution, it is a parliamentary democracy and hereditary monarchy – like many other countries in the European Union. The head of state is the Grand Duke, who appoints the government. There are 60 members of parliament, which is newly elected every five years. Luxembourg has over 500,000 inhabitants, the majority of whom live in the southern half of the country. The capital is also located here with its nearly 92,000 inhabitants (142,000 including the surrounding towns). The second-largest city (28,800 inhabitants) is Esch-sur-Alzette in the traditional industrial region of the southwest. Luxembourg has long been an immigration country with a growing number of foreigners, approximately 43 percent at present. Most of them are Portuguese at a good 37 percent, followed by the French (14 percent), Italians (9 percent), Belgians (8 percent), Germans (6 percent) and the British and Dutch. There are an additional 7,500 foreign employees of the European institutions headquartered in the Grand Duchy and approximately 138,000 border commuters from the neighbouring countries of France, Belgium and Germany. At approximately € 75,000, the per capita income is Europe's, if not the world's, highest. Nearly half of all employees work in the financial sector, 19.9 percent in commerce, transport and communications, 15.4 percent in other service sectors, 10.7 percent in industry and the energy sectors, 5.4 percent in construction and 0.5 percent in agriculture.

The Obersauer dam built in 1957 is near Esch-sur-Sûre. Both the town and the lake are part of Obersauer Natural Park. The recreational area round about the lake invites visitors to bathe, sail and hike.

Along with Brussels and Strasbourg, Luxembourg is one of the three capitals of the European Union, with the headquarters of these EU institutions located in the Centre Européen on the Kirchberg plateau:
– the Secretariat of the European Parliament, which prepares parliamentary tasks,
– the Directorate-General of the European Commission, which deals with the coordination and execution of community policy,
– the European Court of Auditors, which examines all income and expenditures of the European budget,
– the European Investment Bank, which supports the balanced development of the community of states by financing important projects while complying with strict rules of bank management,
– the European Court of Justice, with the Court of First Instance and the European Union Civil Service Tribunal, which ensure the uniform interpretation of European law.

Media centre Luxembourg

The Luxembourgers get their news from papers in French and German, whereby the latter also often contain articles in French and Luxembourgish, a pleasant blend that we also encounter in magazines and brochures. With a viewing rate of 30 percent daily, the channel RTL Télé Lëtzebuerg, broadcasting in Luxembourgish and German, is the most watched broadcaster.

RTL (in the respective national languages) has been part of daily life in Luxembourg's neighbour countries for decades. The RTL Group was formed in the 1990s by the merger of the parent company Compagnie Luxembourgeoise de Télévision (CLT) with the Ufa belonging to the Bertelsmann group. Its programmes can be directly received via Europe's leading satellite system, ASTRA, which supplies over 107 million European satellite and cable households

with television and radio channels as well as media and internet services. It is operated by SES ASTRA with headquarters in Betzdorf. Culture and the arts are also not small minded in the Grand Duchy. In addition to domestic ensembles and orchestras, the full scope of the cabaret and music scenes, the finest art exhibitions and a copious landscape of museums, all year round Luxembourg invites us to its many festivities and festivals with international stars and darlings of the public. In 1995, Luxembourg was the European Capital of Culture; and again in 2007, this time as the heart of the greater region consisting of Luxembourg, Saarland, Rhineland-Palatinate, Lorraine and Wallonia. The programmes available are overwhelming with 450 events from all possible fields. Almost one third of them have been created as cross-border partnerships and concepts. All of the partners have benefited from the confidence and carefulness with which the Luxembourgers aided the cooperation in these projects and brought them to success through their profound knowledge of the neighbouring cultures.

Pages 22/23:
In the year 1900, Grand Duke Adolphe laid the foundation stone for the bridge that bears his name: the 153-metre (502-foot) long Pont Adolphe. It spans the Pétrusse and connects Luxembourg's Old Town with the Gare quarter.

Pages 24/25:
Castle Vianden in the Ardennes was erected on the foundations of a Roman fort and a Carolingian refuge. In 1977, the state purchased the castle, which had fallen to ruin, and had it generously and expertly restored.

Luxembourg City – metropolis of contrasts

Grund is one of the lower districts of Luxembourg City on the riverbank of the Alzette. In the middle ages, this is where millers, tanners, dyers and wool carders settled, who needed the water to carry out their crafts. After the Second World War, immigrants from Italy and Portugal brought Latin flair to the quarter and today well to do Luxembourgers fancy the pretty little houses and their idyllic location.

The Romans knew what they were doing when, in the 4th century, they built two roads that ran across the terrain of today's capital city, and set a watchtower on the Bock Fiels. 600 years later, the Ardennes Count Siegfried built the castle Lucilinburhuc upon its ruins for the same strategic reasons as the Romans before him. The castle attracted commerce and trade and, over the centuries, developed into a mighty stronghold. Under its protection, the city of Luxembourg grew up closely packed on the plateau and along the river valley. When the fortress was razed in the 19th century, this made room for buildings that would reflect the dynamics and prestige of the rising industrial age while at the same time, generous parks were laid out in the heart of the city that many another city may envy. The city has maintained this balance between diligent busyness and languorous reflection. A stop to rest at one of the many charming café patios makes the postmodern grandiosity of banking palaces seem from another world. One can window shop at the usual high-class designer fashion and furniture shops, yet a true explorer can still find charming boutiques. Moreover, when it comes to pleasures of the table, a generous assortment of eateries ensures variety, both for the palate and the pocketbook. It ranges from rightly praised gourmet temples to cuisines from around the world to trendy restaurants and earthy pubs. Culturally, one need not starve either, as Luxembourg City constantly offers new surprises – just as one would expect of a city whose old town and fortress were put on the UNESCO list of World Heritage Sites.

The large, tree-shaded rectangle of the Place des Armes is a popular meeting place. In olden days, Luxembourg's soldiers paraded on the plaza, today it is the site of peaceful multilingual banter, which the waiters in the colourful street cafés master competently.

Left-hand page:
The "Cercle Municipal" – as the Luxembourgers commonly call the city hall on the Place des Armes – is adorned by a façade frieze depicting the delivery of the charter of liberty to the citizens of the city by Countess Ermesinde in the year 1244. The administrative building, which contains a number of festival halls, served as the meeting place of the European Coal and Steel Community (ECSC) from 1953 until 1969.

Whether for tender flirtations or tough business transactions, intimate gossip or a rest for tired feet after a stroll through town, the Place des Armes is always a good tip. Here you can spend quiet time alone or in the company of others and still enjoy the lively surroundings at a cool drink, a first rate espresso, an exquisite snack or a delicious meal.

29

After the order was dissolved, the Jesuits left the city in 1773. Five years later, Empress Maria Theresia, ruler over the Austrian Netherlands, to which Luxembourg then belonged, gave the church to the city as parish church. During the turmoil of the French Revolution, the stirring statue of the Madonna was placed on the high altar to comfort the afflicted.

Left-hand page:
The three towers of the Cathédrale Notre-Dame are landmarks of the Luxembourg skyline. The church, dedicated in 1621, originally belonged to the Jesuit order and combines elements of the Late Gothic, Renaissance and Baroque styles. The opulently decorated alabaster chancel screen and the statues of the founder of the order Ignazio de Loyola and the Mother of God on the main portal are works by Daniel Müller from Freiberg in Saxony.

In 1870, the Grand Duchy was raised to the rank of an autonomous archbishopric and the church of Notre Dame to a cathedral, which was expanded in the 1930s. The royal burial vault is the resting place of John the Blind, Count of Luxembourg and King of Bohemia. Members of the Grand Ducal family are also buried there.

Right:
In the lower quarter of Grund, the National Natural History Museum offers exciting material for young and old. We learn about geology, evolution and the environment. An interactive multimedia system and a nature database encourage scientific curiosity.

ANCIEN HOSPICE SAINT-JEAN
FONDE A CET ENDROIT EN 1308
PAR HENRI VII DE LUXEMBOURG ET MARGUERITE DE BRABANT
RECONSTRUIT EN 1674
PAR LES RELIGIEUSES DE SAINTE ELISABETH
QUI L'ONT DESSERVI JUSQU'EN 1843
ANNEE DU TRANSFERT AU PFAFFENTHAL

Below:
It was not by coincidence that the French-American sculptor Niki de Saint-Phalle (1930–2002) named her blithely stout, brightly coloured female figure of 1995 "Grande Tempérance." It genially contrasts to the more temperate building behind it on the Place Emile Hamilius.

Above:
Four stately, well-restored townhouses are the suitable accommodation for the Museum of Municipal History. The development of Luxembourg since its beginnings in the 10th century is fascinating and builds bridges to our own history.

Left:
The Dicks-Lentz Monument on Jan Pallach Square was erected in 1903 to honour the two Luxembourg poets Edmond de la Fontaine, also known as Dicks (1823–1891), and Michel Lentz (1820–1893). Lentz wrote the lyrics of the national anthem.

33

Above right and below:
A stroll through town always offers new outlooks and insights, particularly on Rue de St. Esprit (above), where the well-maintained homes are quite impressive. Rue de la Congrégation (below), on Place Clairefontaine, presents lovely 19th century-style architecture.

Right-hand page:
Place Clairefontaine lies in the centre of town between the cathedral and parliament. The name originates from the former Clairefontaine Abbey in Arlon, Belgium. The abbey had a sanctuary here, on this site, which was demolished in 1933.

Left and far left:
The "Gëlle Fra" (Golden Lady) on the Place de la Constitution was erected in 1923 in memory of the people of Luxembourg who fell in the First World War. The original sculpture was destroyed by the German occupying forces in 1940. In 1984, it was rebuilt as a symbol of Luxembourg resistance and the sacrifices suffered to regain its freedom.

Left:
Water-spouting grotesques adorn the fountain of the National Library.

Left-hand page:
William II of Orange-Nassau, King of the Netherlands and Grand Duke of Luxembourg is immortalized on the Place Guillaume. In the mid-19th century, he gave Luxembourg its first parliamentarian constitution; then one of Europe's most liberal. The pedestal boasts the coats of arms of the house of Orange-Nassau and Luxembourg and of the twelve cantons of the Grand Duchy.

Left and far left:
The town hall of the City of Luxembourg on Place Guillaume was built between 1830 and 1839 in the Neoclassical style. The outside staircase on the square has been flanked by two lions since 1931. Are they animal contrast to the austere façade or the grim sentinels of the municipal administration?

Pages 38/39:
Names stand the test of time, as is proven by the "Knuedler," as the Luxembourgers call Place Guillaume in reference to the knots used by the Franciscan monks who founded a monastery that stood here in the 13th century to tie the belts of their cowls. Every Wednesday and Saturday morning, the square is busy with market activity.

The old herb market where local farmers once offered their products for sale is recalled in the name of a street in the Old Town: Rue du Marché aux Herbes. A model of this old market can be viewed in the Museum of Municipal History.

Flower boxes in the windows like these in the Rue du Marché aux Herbes lend a cheery air.

40

Above:
The Rue du Rost was once probably something like Luxembourg's barbecue lane, where one could buy crispy grilled meats on a spit. Today, the food here is good still, not at a stand, but in inviting restaurants.

Left:
The Rue du Marché aux Herbes on the old herb market is also still committed to things of the palate and is a good place to take a culinary journey through the world's cuisines, as offered by the capital city of the Grand Duchy.

Right-hand page:
The buildings in the Old Town are genteel and elegant sights, so are often ideal for shops and museums. Those who wish to take a relaxing stroll through the Old Town are best off leaving their cars in a car park at the edge of town and taking public transport.

Right:
Today, the former officers' casino houses the Forum d'art contemporain. International exhibitions offer fascinating insights into the artistic work of mainly young artists.

Right:
Window-shopping on Luxembourg's streets reveals the discreet charm of top-level international luxury. The Grand Duchy has the world's highest per capita income, which guarantees good sales of upper price range goods.

Far right:
The mannequins are cool black and white, as the fashion currently requires. The buyers are probably already busy planning the season after the next. Will it be pastels or bright colours? Whimsical or classic cuts? Experts need to know long in advance to keep their fashion-conscious customers happy.

Grand Ducal
family (hi)stories

When William III of Nassau, King of the Netherlands and Grand Duke of Luxembourg passed away in 1890 without a male heir, the personal union that had existed between the Netherlands and Luxembourg also came to an end. His daughter Wilhelmina did inherit the Dutch throne, but Luxembourg, at that time, could only be ruled by a man. As a result, the Duchy went to the Nassau-Weilburg family line, in the person of the German Duke Adolphe, who, at the age of 73, became Grand Duke Adolphe and the founder of today's dynasty. Upon the death of his son William, who had been blessed with six daughters, Luxembourg was, once again, a man short. This time, without any ado, the law was changed to allow female offspring, for want of a male heir, to take the reins. It was thus that William's oldest daughter, Princess Marie-Adélaïde suddenly found herself on the Grand Ducal throne. The young lady, who possessed a mystical leaning and preferred the kingdom of heaven to the management of earthly affairs, abdicated in favour of her sister Charlotte in 1919 and entered an Italian Carmelite convent. With her wisdom and charisma, and with the blessings of her people by way of a popular referendum in the dynasty's favour, Princess Charlotte became an energetic sovereign. Her marriage to Prince Felix of Bourbon-Parma, which produced two sons and four daughters, was also quite popular with the Luxembourg people. For 45 years, the Grand Duchess oversaw her country – in good times as well as bad. When, in spite of the nation's neutrality, German troops entered and occupied Luxembourg in May 1940, she took her family and her government into exile, joining the Allies in London and supporting her people's resistance movement from there. Upon her return in April 1945, she was jubilantly received by the population, and acclaimed as a symbol of the nation's unity. In 1961, she proclaimed her eldest son, Prince Jean, regent before abdicating in his favour in 1964. She retired to Fischbach Castle, where she passed away on 9 July 1985.

Royal progeny

Following the example of his mother, Grand Duke Jean took care from the earliest days to prepare his son Henri (born in 1955) for his duties as head of state. Henri went to school in Luxembourg and France, and in 1980 obtained a degree in political science from the University of Geneva. This was followed by a time of prac-

tical training in a number of foreign lands, and in 1998, he was proclaimed regent by his father. While a student in Geneva, the young Hereditary Grand Duke had met and fallen in love with a fellow scholar. Maria Teresa Mestre was born in Cuba in 1956, emigrated to New York with her parents in 1959, and later moved to Switzerland. Their marriage in 1981 made her the Hereditary Princess of Luxembourg and then Grand Duchess upon Henri's accession to the throne on 7 October 2000. Today, Her Royal Highness dedicates much time as a special ambassador for UNESCO. She is, as well, the chair of both the foundation that she created with her husband, dedicated the social integration of disabled people, and of the Luxembourg Red Cross. All five of the ruling couple's children were born in the Grand Duchess Charlotte Obstetric Clinic. Three of them, Guillaume (born 1981), Félix (1984) and Louis (1986), have already left home for university, while Alexandra (1991) and Sébastien (1992) still attend school. All of them, of course, speak Luxembourgish, French, German and English plus a little Spanish they learned from their mother. They are very much like other young people their age, differing only in that their godparents are listed in the "Almanach de Gotha" and their portraits hang in many shop windows, the sight of which may make the Luxembourgers sigh: "My, haven't the children grown!" There is hardly any media hype surrounding this Royal Family. When a prince who is barely twenty years old endows his parents with a grandson, they take the happy news with a smile.

Left:
Grand Duchess Charlotte (1896–1985) guided Luxembourg's fate from 1919 until 1964, when she abdicated in favour of her oldest son Jean, father of the present Grand Duke, and retired to Fischbach castle.

Above:
The Palais grand-ducal (Grand Ducal Palace) was built in the second half of the 16th century in the Spanish Renaissance style. Until 1795, the building served as town hall. It was not renovated as the official residence of the Grand Duke until 1890.

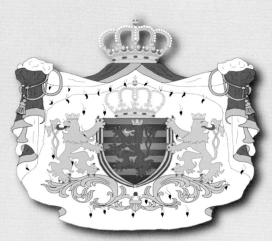

Right, from top to bottom: *The centre of the state coat of arms is formed by a shield in silver and blue with a red lion. Above it is the crown of the Grand Duke – merely a symbol, as Luxembourg's grand dukes do not wear a crown.*

William II ruled as King of the Netherlands and Grand Duke of Luxembourg from 1840 until his death in 1849. This equestrian statue was made in 1844.

Grand Duchess Charlotte presided over her people for four and a half decades with prudence, courage and charisma. The Luxembourgers honoured her with a statue on the Place Clairefontaine.

The Palais grand-ducal, which was extensively renovated between 1992 and 1996, is the office of Grand Duke Henri, where the head of state exercises his official functions.

Left-hand page:
Under Article 44 of the Constitution, the Grand Duke has two principle residences: the Palais grand-ducal, here in the Old Town of Luxembourg City – containing his offices, which are open to visitors from mid-July until late August – and Berg Castle in the centre of the country.

The Grand Ducal Palace fits harmoniously into the cityscape of old Luxembourg. The sandstone walls of the former town hall housed one of the world's most powerful men of the age during his visit in 1541: Holy Roman Emperor Charles V.

Only the sentries in front of the palace signalize that the Grand Duke is here going about his official business. That's all; a big falderal is not customary for Luxembourg.

Pages 48/49:
Luxembourg's Old Town seen from the valley. It's no wonder that the excellent strategic location always tempted conquerors in the past. While commanders spoke of it as the "Gibraltar of the North," more peace-loving voices called it "Europe's loveliest balcony."

The two-storey castle bridge (Pont du Château) was completed in the year 1735. Allusions to the architecture of the Roman Empire are unmistakable. Nearby Trier, an outpost of Roman culture and trade in the Moselle region founded as "Augusta Treverorum" by Caesar Augustus shortly before the turn of the last millennium, long stood in the architectural memory of the region.

Pages 50/51:
An almost Mediterranean scene: tidy terrace gardens nestle at the feet of the steep cliffs, which protect them from the harsh winds and collect the sun's warm rays for their benefit. Even Johann Wolfgang von Goethe – who seems to have travelled everywhere – was delighted at his visit to endearing Luxembourg.

Right and far right:
The small bridge leading over the Alzette at the foot of the fortress walls (right) is called the "Stierchen." The fortress on the Bock Fiels was razed at the end of the 19th century, yet the rock is still worth discovering. For one, there's a wonderful view from up here to the Old Town and the lower quarter of Grund, and secondly this is where the entrance to the Bock casements is located, a true underground city that was drilled as deep as 40 metres (130 feet) into the mountain under Austrian rule between 1737 and 1746.

The trees on the shore are reflected in the Alzette, one of the country's four largest rivers besides the Moselle, Sauer and Our. From Grund, an idyllic shoreline path takes you by foot or bicycle to Hesperange 5 kilometres (3 miles) south of the capital with its suspension bridge over the river.

Pages 54/55:
From the Bock Fiels, our eyes sweep the lower district of Grund with its lovely little houses and the abbey of Neumünster. The historic complex is one of the most important in the city of Luxembourg.

53

Pages 56/57:
Construction on a convent
in Luxembourg-Pfaffenthal
was begun in 1687 by the
sisters of the Clarisses-
Urbanistes du St-Esprit
order. In 1842 it was
rededicated as a hospice.
The senior citizens who
live here enjoy a wonderful
view of the Old Town.

Right:
Four hundred years ago,
the first abbey – the old
minster – was replaced by
a new Benedictine abbey:
Neumünster. When France
annexed Luxembourg
as a département after
the French Revolution,
the monks were forced
to leave.

Above:
Cells being plentiful, the
former abbey of Neu-
münster served as a
prison until 1984. After
extensive restorations and
modernization, it opened
its portals again in 2004
as an international meet-
ing place with the goal
of promoting dialogue
between cultures and a
culture of dialogue.

Above:
Grund's once affordable rents attracted Italian and Portuguese guest workers on their arrival. They implemented the dialogue of cultures from the outset by bringing their lifestyles into the quarter. Today, the lovely cottages on the banks of the Alzette are prized real estate.

Right:
If you look close enough, you'll find many a cosy niche in the quarter of Grund. Demand for one of the comfortable homes or snazzy offices in these endearing surroundings is increasing and raising the real estate prices sky high.

Above:
Grund has managed
to preserve its homey
character, even if the fresh
plaster sometimes covers
up the most impressive
histories.

Left:
Congenial chic pub
ambience, paradise for
night owls, these are other
features of Grund: more
good reasons to stop by.

Pages 62/63:
View of the Kirchberg
plateau, Luxembourg's
European quarter, head-
quarters of important
institutions of the Euro-
pean Union. After the
construction frenzy of past
decades, it is gradually
adopting a distinct blend
of urbanism and architec-
tural design.

WELL-GUARDED INVESTMENTS

Something like 160 banks are headquartered in the Grand Duchy; mergers and new establishments keep the numbers fairly consistent. In addition, there are impressive and increasing numbers of pension funds, investment and reinsurance firms, et al. Luxembourg holds position no. 1 in the EU for private banking and no. 2 in the world for fund business, after the USA.

What makes Luxembourg so attractive for financiers? Bankers can explain it best. A renowned banking corporation with branches in Luxembourg offers these incentives of the country to any interested new blood: it is not only located in the heart of Europe (that always sounds good, but one asks oneself how many hearts Europe can have) and the headquarters of a number of EU institutions (including the European Investment Bank and the European Court of Justice), it also offers advantageous prerequisites due to its finance laws, its strictly-kept banking secrecy, and the prohibition of money-laundering. Moreover, good understandings with the relevant authorities are enjoyed, which helps to save time in receiving approval for new offers on the market.

The less red tape, the more favourable it is in the international competition of financial institutions. Then there is the fact that Luxembourg was the first member state to adopt the 1985 EC investments directive as national law. This means that funds that make their home in the Grand Duchy can travel freely throughout the European Union – similarly to those citizens whose countries signed the Schengen Agreement. Schengen, which also happens to be a lovely winemaking village, with the remnants of a 13th century castle and a palace with Baroque gardens, situated in the border triangle where Luxembourg meets Germany and France, has a monument to remind us of 14 June 1985. It was on that day, on a ship on the Moselle, that representatives of an initial five EC member states placed their signatures upon the agreement to abolish border controls and introduce free movement of persons and goods.

It's only money

Money is merchandise; if it weren't, those in the banking business would not speak of "products." And in order to sell and move such products, connections are worth their weight in gold. Luxembourg City – small in size, large in prestige, where giants of international finance stand shoulder to shoulder and even a lame cat could go from one bank to the next in a downpour and not get wet – is an ideal springboard for any charming and ambitious young banker who hopes to prove their mobility (and must, to last in the business). Not only while engaging in multi-lingual chitchat in the corridors or bending over their books, but even long after ordinary office hours, the work goes on with dedication to the profession in order to earn one's advancement. Polishing the social parquet, milling about in the milieu of bars, eateries and events, the places to "be" or to meet for a tête-à-tête and, later, in the select private clubs, which accept only those who are beginning to matter. The proof of a successful PR tour of this sort, says the insider to the novice, is when, at the drop of a name, the matching face instantaneously appears. The formula is impressively simple – and likewise fierce.

According to statistics, 30,000 jobs in Luxembourg are spread amongst the diverse financial sectors. The Grand Duchy has one of the world's highest per-capita incomes. Yet, even in Luxembourg, the purchasing power of the salaries in the service sector or in industry is limited. The country has top earners and welfare recipients, like every country. It is an open secret that, at the end of the day, it is foreign investors whose pockets are jingling; a result, they assert, of the agreeable conditions offered them: as sweet and as tempting as candy.

Left:
Paper bank notes are the same in all euro countries. They were designed by the Austrian Robert Kalina and portray fictional buildings with characteristic architectural European styles, ranging from the ancient classical to modern steel and glass structures.

Above:
The ingenious lighting system of the Deutsche Bank was designed by the firm of Peter Anders. It is aligned to the requirements of each individual employee and automatically adapts to the outdoor light.

Above right:
The branch office of the Deutsche Bank based on the blueprints of the German architect Gottfried Böhm is located in Luxembourg's European quarter on the Boulevard Konrad Adenauer.

Centre right:
Harmonious shapes and transparency are the distinguishing features of the Hypovereinsbank building on the Kirchberg plateau, which was designed by Pierluigi Lanini.

Right:
Old and new architectural splendour stand in lovely harmony on the Boulevard Royal.

Pages 66/67:
The Luxembourg Philhar-
monic Orchestra, formed
in 1996 from the orchestra
of Radio Luxembourg, is
among Europe's best. It
moved into its new home
on the Place de l'Europe
in Kirchberg in June 2005.
The layout of the white
steel main building is the
shape of an eye sur-
rounded by slim columns,
which lend it rhythm, light
and airiness.

Behind the light-flooded
lobby, the large concert
hall named after Grand
Duchess Charlotte forms
the heart of the philhar-
monic.

The shell-shaped,
radiantly white Salle de
musique de chambre next
to the main building is
devoted to chamber
music.

Right-hand page:
In addition to the arts,
finance and important
European institutions,
Kirchberg is also a
commercial centre, with
trendy shopping centres
and hypermarkets.

Pages 70/71:
The Adolph Bridge
(Pont Adolphe), which
spans the Pétrusse valley
at 42 metres (138 feet),
was built between 1899
and 1903 during the reign
of Grand Duke Adolphe
after plans by the French
engineer Paul Séjourné.

Left-hand page:
After the fortress was razed, a new quarter grew up on the Plateau Bourbon beyond the Pétrusse, in which the historicizing blend of styles of the Wilhelminian age dominated. The tower of the state savings bank has loomed gallantly above the Place de Metz since 1913.

Below and above right :
In the direct vicinity of the Avenue de la Liberté, the palace-like administrative building of the former Arbed steelworks built in 1922 testifies to the former fame and splendour of Luxembourg's heavy industry. Its gables are adorned with the figures of Mercury and Victoria, symbols of successful commerce.

Bottom:
Mother and child, a sculpture by Henry Moore, behind it the headquarters of the Arcelor-Mittal steelworks. Arbed became the Arcelor corporation and merged with the Indian steel giant Mittal in 2006 to become the world's largest steel producer.

Pages 74/75:
Quirinus Chapel, the oldest Christian structure in the city, is a moving fusion of nature and architecture. St. Quirinus was the patron saint of the city of Luxembourg until the mid-17th century, when he was replaced by Mary, the comforter of the afflicted.

Luxembourg – up and down the countryside

In the east of the Grand Duchy, on the German border, the Moselle leisurely winds its way through the landscape, like here near Wormeldange. The Romans called the river the "Mosella" or "little Meuse." The first grapevines arrived in the baggage of the Roman legions.

From the austere beauty of the dense forests, broad plateaus and deeply gouged valleys of the Ardennes to the bizarre rock formations of the Müllerthal – or Little Switzerland and the gentle slopes and loops of the Moselle, when it comes to landscapes, the Grand Duchy has plenty to offer all the way from north to south. The "Gutland" as the southern part is called – it's also referred to as Luxembourg's orchard – stretches to the west and the east of the capital between the Red Land, the Müllerthal and the Moselle and is a hikers' paradise. In the valleys of the Mamer, Eisch and Alzette, fauna and flora are still unspoilt. Scores of lovingly restored villages, such as Useldange, which received the Europa Nostra Award for revitalization of its historic centre, welcome visitors. Ansembourg Castle and its gardens in the Valley of the Seven Castles are well worth a detour, as well as the enchanting Baroque church in Koerich, the keep of Hollenfels (the castle is a youth hostel today), St Michael's Tower in nearly 2000-year-old Mersch, the potter village of Nospelt or Bourglinster, where the castle provides a festive framework year round for concerts. You mustn't miss the prehistoric caves near Schoenfels in the Mamer valley and the remains of the Villa Marisca – an imposing Roman estate – in Mersch. Other sights include the Fond-de-Gras Industrial and Railway Park, an open-air museum preserving memories of the Industrial Age (a rolling mill, a collier's pub, corner shop, operating collier and steam railway). In Bettembourg, ten kilometres (6 miles) south of the capital, is "Parc merveilleux" a fairy tale park for young and old: fairy tale scenes, an enclosure with domestic animals and more exotic creatures, miniature golf, a miniature railway, pony express, playground and picnic areas. It also has aquariums, terrariums and vivariums that present the diverse species of the Amazon rainforest and African desert regions. How about a game of Pétanque in the castle garden for some exercise and fun?

Left-hand page:
Sixteenth century arcades and the warm colours of the façades make a stroll through the old winegrowing village of Wellenstein a visual delight. Sturdy hikers will discover their pleasure while roaming through the vineyards.

Left:
Another asset: in addition to its well-kept winegrowers' houses, lively Wellenstein also is home to the country's largest cooperative wine cellar.

Far left:
Fountains, like this one in Wellenstein, ripple everywhere in the Grand Duchy. Whether simple or majestic, they emit joie de vivre and contemplativeness. Time trickles past; we remain as we are, they seem to be murmuring – based loosely on the national motto.

Left:
Small discoveries that are not necessarily listed in the travel guides are everywhere to be found on the roadsides. An ounce of curiosity, a friendly question and all of a sudden, you're involved in a conversation offering some surprising firsthand titbits about the country and its people.

Left:
Like all the other wine-growing towns on the Moselle, Ehnen can also be described as "picturesque" and "historic" and rightly so. The Wine Museum, an informative documentary and cultural centre focused on viniculture, is especially enlightening.

Above:
The Romans called the town of Remich on the Moselle "Remacum". As pioneers of road building, they would not have been surprised that one day the Trans-European road network between Saarbrücken and Luxembourg City would pass through here.

81

Above:
In the cool vaults of a wine cellar like this one in Remich, the temperature remains constant both summer and winter. This ensures that the wine can mature and develop its bouquet without thermal shock.

Right:
Most vineyards have been owned by the same family for generations. Professional expertise is learned very early through watching, lending a hand, testing and tasting.

Far right:
Luxembourg's Moselle produces primarily white wines. The assortment is augmented by fruity reds, rosés, and Crémant du Luxembourg, a festive sparkling wine.

Above:
The fertile and heavy soils in the canton of Remich deliver well-rounded wines with harmonious bouquets while the limestone soil in the canton of Grevenmacher results in more racy and elegant wines. The delicious liquid rests in big-bellied barrels until being bottled.

Left:
The foam that flows into the glass like cream gave Crémant its name.

Pages 84/85:
Riesling thrives especially well on the shell lime soils on the slopes above Wormeldange.

83

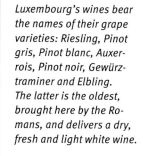

Left-hand page:
Chapels for quiet prayer, like this one on the Kreuzerberg near Wormeldange, are a common sight in the vineyards. The flag of the Grand Duchy waves high above the left Moselle bank, in the valley a bridge links Wormeldange with Wincheringen on the German shore.

Luxembourg's winegrowing region stretches over 40 kilometres (25 miles) from Schengen in the south to Wasserbillig. It is among the northernmost in Europe. The fact that the country's wines nevertheless possess character lies in the region's favourable, particularly mild microclimate.

Luxembourg's wines bear the names of their grape varieties: Riesling, Pinot gris, Pinot blanc, Auxerrois, Pinot noir, Gewürztraminer and Elbling. The latter is the oldest, brought here by the Romans, and delivers a dry, fresh and light white wine.

Pages 88/89:
Ehnen is a tiny village on the Moselle with an historic village centre. Some of the houses standing in a row about the church were built in the 15th to 18th centuries. The church was rebuilt in 1826 and is the only round church in Luxembourg today.

"FOOD AND DRINK HOLD BODY AND SOUL TOGETHER"

Luxembourg's cuisine reflects the geography and history of the country in a delightful way. "What the land has to offer" is the basis of the manifold fare, nurtured by the inventiveness needed in days when the cupboard was bare, and the influence of the French gastronomique. We can enjoy home-style sausages and pastries enhanced with Riesling; smoked ham from the Ardennes with the characteristic flavours of beech and oak; game and mushroom specialities; well-bred beef, mutton and pork; pike, trout and eel. Thanks to the restoration of the water quality, the "Kriepsen" (crayfish) which once abounded have returned to many streams, but as yet only in modest numbers, so imports are still needed for the traditional Luxembourg-style crayfish dish, served in a vegetable-Riesling stock. The markets, with their profusion of crisp fruits and vegetables and the entire panoply of domestic kitchen herbs, are a welcome sight. The bakeries release the fragrance of crusty baguettes and crunchy wholemeal loaves, and many a sweet tooth is tempted by the plentiful offerings of the pastry shops and "confiseries": delicate treats that melt on the tongue, damson and yellow plum cakes fresh from the oven, fine chocolate and exquisite confectionery that testify to a love of indulgence. The selection and quality of the Italian ice cream parlours compares to that found in the home country. The Grand Duchy's national dish is called "Judd mat Gaardebounen": smoked pork blade over broad beans in a Riesling and Silvaner gravy; substantial and hearty, simmered slowly, then sprinkled with finely crushed summer savoury. The traditional side dish is boiled potatoes, "gegréifte Gromperen." With the exception of the flowery Gewürztraminer, every Luxembourg wine suits this meal, but it also goes well with a hearty, domestic draught beer.

The "Friture," a classic on the menus of the inviting restaurants on the shores of the Moselle, should be accompanied by a first-rate Riesling. Small river fish, briefly marinated in lemon juice and then rolled in flour, are served up fresh from the deep-fryer, salted and peppered. It's no crime to eat them with your fingers; they taste even better that way. They are a pleasurable way to end a jaunt to the picturesque winegrowing villages above the river, or a cycle ride on the bike paths along its shore, or even a lazy steamboat excursion for a waterview of the vineyards on the Luxembourg and German hillsides.

The juice of the grape

Wine, a delicious legacy from Roman days, is the crop grown most along the Moselle. In olden days, the grapes grew as far as the gates of Luxembourg City; today's cultivation is focused on the slopes above the bends of the Moselle, a "wine belt" (Wäistrooss), 42 kilometres (26 miles) in length, from Schengen in the south to Wasserbillig in the north. The wine museum in Ehnen is worth a visit, as are the many wine festivals, while cellars and estates alike offer tastings and expert advice. Nine grape varieties give their names to the choice white Luxembourg wines. These include the light and refreshing Elbling; the mild and mellow Rivaner; the elegant Pinot blanc; the full-bodied, if not fervent, Pinot gris for aperitif and dessert; and Riesling, considered "king of wines" by many, with its subtle fruity bouquet. Those who do not favour white wine will appreciate the aromatic Pinot noir, which can be enjoyed as a red or rosé. The champagne-method "crémant de Luxembourg," named for the creamy foam that flows into the glass, is a favourite for all celebrations.

Like the quality wines, Luxembourg's fruit brandies also bear the prized seal, "Marque Nationale." The grand catalogue of liquids 70-proof and above ranges from apple to mulberry, yellow plum and damson. And if alcohol is spurned, you can still indulge in fresh grape and apple juice. Either way: "Gesondheet!"

Left:
A breakfast as in France: a fragrant croissant and a cup of strong espresso are a favourite duo.

Above:
Leisure over stress: the first lunch guests have found their way to the Place Guillaume II. The large square in the centre of the capital city is enlivened by a colourful market two mornings a week.

Right, from top to bottom: *Many castles and palaces have cafeterias or even, as here in Bourglinster, a castle tavern.*

Tangy Ardennes ham on freshly grated raw vegetables is low in calories and high in delight.

A hearty "choucroute," like that to be had in Alsace: various cuts of pork served over white wine sauerkraut and boiled potatoes are accompanied perfectly by a glass of Riesling or a cool beer.

Deep-fried river fish are a classic dish in the handsome taverns along the Moselle. They are preferably eaten with the fingers.

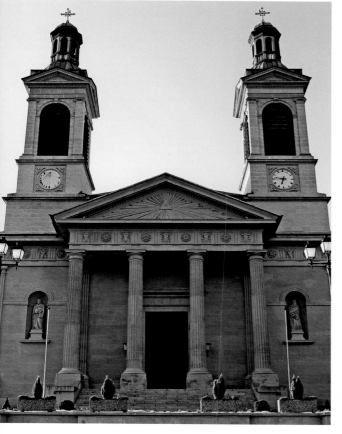

Left-hand page:
St. Michael's Tower of the town of Mersch stands on the square of the same name, Place St. Michel. It is all that remains of the old church. The mother of Dutch King William III advocated its preservation in 1851.

Far left:
The Late Neoclassical double spires of the parish church tower over the town of Mersch.

Left:
Today, the castle of Mersch houses the municipal administration.

Left:
Useldange, situated on the Attert, is towered over by its castle ruins. The village was granted the Europa Nostra Award for cultural heritage.

93

A few kilometres before the Moselle bends to the east to leaves Luxembourg, it flows past Grevenmacher. The town was granted its charter in the year 1252, and has been the cantonal and district capital since 1839.

Right-hand page:
Battle observer Goethe stopped by in Grevenmacher in 1792. The famous "Cannonade of Valmy" in northeastern France, of which he was an eyewitness, ended with the retreat of the Prussian-Austrian coalition and the advance by the French revolutionary army on the Rhine.

Winegrowing, commerce and small trade are the main sources of employment in the little town of about 4,200 inhabitants, in addition to tourism and industry. The Old Town of Grevenmacher with its narrow alleyways and the remains of medieval fortifications is worth exploration.

KOFFERSCHMATTS
GÄSSEL

Echternach (Iechternach) was granted its charter in 1236, but its documented history goes back far earlier. The Anglo-Saxon missionary Willibrord from Northumbria founded an abbey here in the year 698. The picturesque town lies on the Sûre (Sauer), which forms the border to Germany here, and is the gateway to Luxembourg's Little Switzerland.

Right-hand page:
The Old High German word "Thing" means something like assembly. The Echternach Dingstuhl (Dënzelt) of 1444, an especially beautiful example of secular Gothic architecture, was originally the seat of the lay assessor court; today it is the meeting place of the town council.

The abbey of Echternach became famous in the middle ages as a centre of outstanding manuscript illumination. Among the works of art created by the monks is the Golden Gospels of Echternach ("Codex Aureus Epternacensis") from the 11th century, which is kept in the German National Museum in Nuremberg.

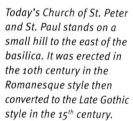

Pages 98/99:
The Echternach Benedic-
tine abbey is situated in
the middle of a garden
with fountains, a Rococo
pavilion and orangerie.
The abbey museum in
the vaulted cellar offers a
look at the history of the
monastery and the Echter-
nach School of medieval
book illumination.

Today's Church of St. Peter
and St. Paul stands on a
small hill to the east of the
basilica. It was erected in
the 10th century in the
Romanesque style then
converted to the Late Gothic
style in the 15th century.

On the southwestern
periphery of Echternach,
the two-storey, palace-like
manor house of a Roman
estate was excavated in
1975–76. The farm lying
in the midst of extensive
acreage was among the
largest and wealthiest in
the perimeters of the
Roman provincial capital
Augusta Treverorum (Trier).

Left-hand page:
Willibrord had the first,
Merovingian church built
in Echternach about the
year 700, around 800 it
was replaced by a Carolin-
gian structure with a crypt.
In the 11th century, its
place was taken by the
Romanesque basilica of
Saint Willibrord. It was
destroyed during the Bat-
tle of the Bulge and rebuilt
after the war.

"Little Switzerland," part of the Germano-Luxembourg Nature Park, stretches between the Sauer and the Black Ernz. Its huge, bizarre sandstone formations, its grottoes, ravines, gaps and walls marked by the wind and weather stimulate the imagination and wanderlust. The paths lead through majestic beech forests, the eyes are soothed by the gently rolling panorama, then by a stream happily snaking its way through the meadows.

Pages 104/105:
To the north of Ettelbrück, high above the Sûre, sits enthroned one of the most imposing castles between the Rhine and Meuse. Castle Bourglinster mouldered to ruins until it was bought by the state in 1972 and restored. Today it invites visitors with a sophisticated cultural programme.

Protected fauna and flora, forest stillness and nature's might, like that of the three-streamed waterfall of the Black Ernz roaring into the lake below, handsome towns, old castles and churches, make the Müllerthal a popular destination. The steep cliffs tempt many a climber to conquer them.

Pages 106/107:
Velz, Rupes, Larochette: whether in German, Latin or French, the medieval castle was always named after its location on a rock above the White Ernz. The town of Larochette, once an important centre of the textile industry, is a popular destination on the edge of Little Switzerland.

In 1248, the powerful counts of Vianden founded an abbey for the order of the Trinitarians in the town at the feet of their castle. The cloister, used by the monks for their meditation, has been preserved. The attached Trinitarian church is one of Luxembourg's most beautiful Gothic buildings.

Vianden is a lively, endearing little town, in which the glorious past and openness to new forms of artistic expression harmoniously complement one another – a perfect example of Luxembourg savoir vivre.

Left-hand page:
Over centuries, the mighty castle of Vianden arose upon the remains of Roman and Carolingian fortifications on a cliff above the Our valley in the Ardennes. Excellently restored, it offers a perfect example of how chivalrous society lived in the middle ages.

109

Pages 110/111:
The little Ardennes city of Vianden is among Luxembourg's most visited places. It is located in the northeast on the border to the German state of Rhineland-Palatinate. Vianden was built on both shores of the border river Our. The town, and not the river, forms the border to Germany only here and for a few kilometres.

Left:
The Benedictine Abbey of St. Maurice and St. Maurus in Clervaux in the Ardennes was founded in the early 20th century. Visitors can enter the forecourt, the church, the crypt and view a small exhibition about monastery life.

The castle of Clervaux is among the Grand Duchy's tourism highlights. Its walls also house a museum containing testimonies of the Ardennes offensive, during which the castle was badly damaged, a collection of 22 models of Luxembourg castles and palaces and a toy museum.

The parish church of Clervaux was built between 1910 and 1912 on a rocky ridge close to the castle. It was modelled after the church of the Romanesque monastery of Cluny in Burgundy. The chancel, altars and stations of the cross in the sanctuary are the works of the Aachen sculptor Lambert Piedboeuf.

113

Above:
Ardennes landscape near Doennange to the west of Clervaux with fields, pastures, hiking trails and a view to the far horizon. This sparsely populated region in the north of the Grand Duchy is rugged and scenic. Here and there, we find a small village on the edge of the rural road, otherwise nature itself without a trace of the turbulence of the banking hub.

Right:
In the midst of the forested hills and still river valleys of the Ardennes lies Wiltz, a city of charm and a rich history. Castle Wiltz dates from the 18th century and has served as the backdrop for an internationally renowned open-air festival every summer since 1953.

114

Pages 116/117:
From romantic Esch-sur-Sûre, the pathway leads up to the castle ruins, the oldest sections of which date from the 10th century. There we are offered a magical panorama view of the still course of the river.

Left:
Clervaux Castle – superbly restored with government aid from the ruins left by the German bombardment during the Battle of the Bulge.

Below:
With its approximately 42-kilometre (26-mile) shoreline, the reservoir in the Upper Sûre Nature Park is Luxembourg's most important standing water body.

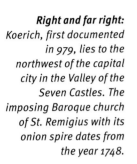

Right and far right:
Koerich, first documented in 979, lies to the northwest of the capital city in the Valley of the Seven Castles. The imposing Baroque church of St. Remigius with its onion spire dates from the year 1748.

Below:
In the centre of Koerich, the ruins of a huge castle reach to the heavens. The 13th century square structure, originally protected by an over 10-metre (33-foot) wide moat, once possessed a mighty keep, called the "witches' tower."

Picturesque Ansembourg in the Eisch valley, the Valley of the Seven Castles, is crowned by a bastion built in the 12th century. In the valley, a few hundred metres from the town, Count Lambert of Ansembourg built a smart Baroque palace in the year 1638.

Pages 120/121: Septfontaines in the Valley of the Seven Castles literally means "seven springs." These springs feed the fountains in the town centre. The parish church built on the orders of Thomas von Simmern in 1316–17 combines Romanesque and Gothic stylistic elements.

STRAIGHT FROM A FAIRY TALE – LUXEMBOURG'S CASTLES

Luxembourg has no dearth of castles. They sit enthroned upon rocks and rise above river courses, proud and defiant as in a picture book. Castles were protection from enemies, housing the defenders and the local population during an attack. One imposing example of this was the mighty Lützelburg on Bock Fiels high above the rivers Alzette and Pétrusse, which gave the city and the nation their names. Over the centuries, successive sovereigns expanded it to become a massive over- and underground stronghold, bringing it fame as a "Gibraltar of the North." The many kilometres of casemates, worked into the stone in the 18th century by the Austrians under Empress Maria Theresia, accommodated soldiers, horses, munitions and representatives of trades that were crucial to survival (bakers, cooks, smiths ...). Long after the aboveground fortress had been razed, its inner recesses offered refuge to the population of the capital city during the battles of the Second World War.

The power of the counts of Vianden, whose influence in the Middle Ages ranged over great territories between the Rhine, Meuse and Moselle, is embodied in the castle built by them which dominates the Our river valley in the northeast of the country. In size alone, it is one of the most significant of its age. It was carefully restored with the aid of considerable government funding and has become one of Luxembourg's favourite tourist sights. In the summertime, Vianden Castle is a grand venue for cultural events. Every August, a weeklong medieval festival, complete with tournaments, banquets and music, demonstrates how the knights of old lived, dined and amused themselves. An excursion to the castle ruins of Stolzembourg to the north of Vianden is also recommended. It is situated on a hill in the centre of the village of the same name, where there is also a copper mine museum offering underground trips with the mining railroad.

Art and culture within historic walls

The whitewashed walls of Clervaux Castle glow under a slate-blue roof. The original twelfth-century fortress burned down during the Battle of the Bulge. Since its reconstruction, it is home to three museums. One commemorates the famous Ardennes battle; another contains a collection of models of Luxembourgian castle architecture. But, Clervaux is most famous for a unique photography collection, "The Family of Man." Edward Steichen, a native Luxembourger who emigrated to the USA in 1881 at the age of two with his parents and became a famous American fashion photographer, assembled it while curator of the photography collection of New York's Museum of Modern Art. It was there that his final selection of 500 photographs – by 270 photographers from approximately 70 countries, both amateurs and luminaries of the profession– was shown for the first time in 1955. Steichen's humanist aspiration was to promote our understanding of one another through the universal language of photography and thus prevent wars. In accordance with Steichen's wishes, the collection was later donated to his homeland.

In every July since 1953, the Renaissance façade of Castle Wiltz in the Oesling has formed the magnificent backdrop for an open-air festival that brings magic moments to lovers of theatre and of all music genres. Premier acting ensembles, orchestras and soloists

Left:
The ruins of Beaufort Castle are located in the limits of the town of Befort. It probably dates from the late 12th century.

Above:
Graceful elegance in the centre of a generous park: the palace in Septfontaines.

guarantee a feast for both the ears and eyes. In the weeks around Pentecost, the surrounding countryside is spattered by bright broom blossoms, which is celebrated by the Wiltz Gënzefest (broom festival) on Whit Monday.

Northwest of the capital, the Eisch meanders through the Valley of the Seven Castles. They, too, are rich in history, like all that you will encounter on your journey through Luxembourg. And let's not neglect the imposing structures built in the centre of Esch-sur-Alzette, the Grand Duchy's second largest city, they are the "castles" with which Luxembourg's knights of the industrial age once commemorated themselves in the styles of Wilhelminian, Jugendstil and Art Deco architecture.

Top right:
The city of Vianden is overlooked by the massive castle fortifications. Much of it was renovated in the past centuries. The castle chapel, with its colourful sanctuary, was restored in the original colours of the Romanesque age.

Centre right:
Portal of Bettendorf Palace on the border between the "Gutland" in the south and the northern "Oesling," the Luxembourg Ardennes.

Right:
Bettendorf Palace: serene, playful to elaborate, year of construction 1728. Outside the town, a memorial trail commemorates the tragic events at the end of the last war.

Pages 124/125:
Mondorf-les-Bains, a renowned spa resort in the southeast of Luxembourg on the border to France and Germany for nearly 150 years, is favoured by a mild microclimate.

Right:
The thermal baths experienced a formidable boom after their purchase by the Luxembourg government in the late 19th century.

Below:
A niece of Charlemagne named Muomina bestowed her possessions to the abbey in Echternach. They included a small village, which from then on was named "Muomendorph" – today's Mondorf-les-Bains.

In the 19th century, the Dutch regime levied salt imports from Holland with a tax, to the chagrin of their Luxembourg subjects. A Mondorf notary discovered that the water from a small brook in the town tasted similarly salty as the Aachen spring water that he had drunken during his regimens there. Drilling commenced and water was discovered at a depth of 415 metres (1,363 feet). The sulphurous liquid was watery gold for Mondorf. Today, the spa gardens are a favourite place for leisurely strolls.

Pages 128/129:
The Neo-Gothic parish church of St. Martin in Dudelange to east of Esch-sur-Alzette is the country's third-largest church. It was built in the late 19th century.

Many call Esch-sur-Alzette in the "Red Land," 18 kilometres (11 miles) south of Luxembourg City, the secret capital. Here in the southwest of the Grand Duchy, important iron ore deposits were discovered in the 19th century. Mines and steelworks were established in the area and Esch grew to become the centre of Luxembourg's heavy industry. The smokestacks puffed while the captains of industry invested in their personal images with the finest Jugendstil structures. Today, Esch has nearly 30,000 inhabitants, more than 50 percent of whom are of immigrant ancestry.

The steel crisis that began in the 1970s was hard on Esch and the surrounding region. The mines closed down and funds for redevelopment of the once so splendid city centre were long lacking. Today, Esch's façades again shine in their former glory and the city is realigning its sights. Service providing businesses and technological firms have settled on the surrounding industrial grounds. Culturally, the city is also at its peak. It has a theatre, a number of outstanding museums, art galleries, libraries, a renowned conservatory and an all-round centre called the "art factory."

131

Neo-Gothic monumentality in Esch-sur-Alzette: the parish and deanship church of St. Joseph easily overshadows even the most ostentatious palaces of the steel magnates. On 14th May 1877, in consideration of the rapidly growing worker population of Esch-sur-Alzettes, the church was dedicated to the more popular St. Joseph; a bitter blow for St. John, who had been the patron of the city since the 16th century. The city's architectural competition for the construction of the church was won by the Luxembourger Charles Arendt, a significant representative of historicism in the region.

Right-hand page:
Charles Arendt was inspired by the cathedral architecture of the High Middle Ages in his plans for the Neo-Gothic church, a chief model being the church of Notre-Dame in Melun to the north of Paris.

INDEX

10 km

BELGIEN

DEUTSCHLAND

Prüm

Houffalize

Hautbellain

Weiswampach

Troisvierges

Asselborn

Heinerscheid

Wincrange

Abb. St.-Maurice ★ ● Clervaux

Munshausen

Oberwampach

Hosingen

Untereisenbach

Eschweiler

Wilwerwiltz

Consthum

Winseler

Putscheid

Keppeshausen

Bastogne

Wiltz

Kautenbach

Schloss ★ ● Vianden

Harlange

Bavigne

Goesdorf

Hoscheid

Bitburg

Barrage de la
Haute-Sûre

Esch-
sur-Sûre

Bourscheid

Fouhren

Boulaide

Neunhausen

Bastendorf

Schloss Gruef ★

Hochfels
460 m ▲

Arsdorf
549 m ▲

Rindschleiden ★

Nieder-
feulen

Diekirch ■

Bettendorf

Reisdorf

Bigonville

Wahl

Petite Suisse

Dillingen

Rambrouch

Grosbous

Mertzig

Ettelbruck ■ Patton-
Museum

Schieren

Ermsdorf

Aleburg ★

Beaufort

Berdorf

Echternach

Bettborn

Vichten

Colmar-
Berg

Medernach

Heringerburg

Waldbillig ★

Abbaye ● Römervilla

Rosport

Ell

Bissen

Nommern

Larochette

Müllerthal ★

Consdorf

Girsterklaus ★

Redange-
sur-Attert

Attert

Useldange

Meysembourg ★

Enz

Girst

Born

LUXEMBURG

Oberpallen

Beckerich

Vallée des sept
Châteaux

Mersch ■

Fischbach

Bech

Mompach

Saeul

Tuntange

Lintgen

Altlinster

Radio
Luxembourg

Biwer

Trier ■

Septfontaines

Arlon ■

Eischen

Hobscheid

Eisch

Lorentz-
weiler

Junglinster ●

Schloss
Bourglinster ★

Manternach

Mertert

Wasserbillig

St. Remigius ★

Koerich

Kehlen

Steinsel

Betzdorf

Mosel

Steinfort

Kopstal ●

Walferdange ●

Grevenmacher ■

Konz

Capellen

Bridel

Niederanven

Syre

Jardin des
Papillons ★

Mamer

Garnich

Strassen ●

Musée Nat.
d'Histoire
et d'Art

Centre
Européen

Flaxweiler

Machtum

Clemency

Bertrange ●

Luxembourg ★

Sandweiler ●

Schuttrange ●

Ahn

Dippach

Cathédrale
Notre-Dame

Casemates

Oetrange

Ehnen

Wormeldange

Saarburg

Bascharage

Leudelange

Itzig

Contern

Reckange-
sur-Mess

Hespérange ●

Weiler-
la-Tour

Stadtbredimus

Pétange ●

Tetelberg ★

Sanem

Parc
Merveilleux ★

Roeser

Alzette

Dalheim

Bous

Caves St. Martin ★

Remich ■

Differdange ●

Soleuvre

Mondercange ●

Ricciacus ★

Longwy ■

Museum des
Widerstandes ★

Schifflange

Bettembourg ■

Frisange

Wellenstein ●

Musée Folklorique
et Viticole ★

Esch-
sur-Alzette ■

Kayl

Hellange

Mondorf-
les-Bains

St. Martin ● Dudelange ■

Burmerange

Rumelange ● Musée Nat.
des Mines ★

Schengen ●

Perl ●

Mettlach ■

FRANKREICH

Hettange

Sierck-
les-Bains ●

Merzig ■

The Chamber of Deputies in Luxembourg City is located next to the Grand Ducal Palace. The Chamber, Luxembourg's parliament, is the legislature of the Grand Duchy of Luxembourg and consists of 60 members.

Credits

Book design
www.hoyerdesign.de

Map
Fischer Kartografie, Aichach

Translation
Faith Gibson Tegethoff, Bonn

All rights reserved

Printed in Germany
Repro by Artilitho snc, Lavis-Trento, Italy
www.artilitho.com
Printed and processed by Offizin Andersen Nexö, Leipzig
© 2011 Verlagshaus Würzburg GmbH & Co. KG
© Photographs: Tina and Horst Herzig
© Texts: Sylvia Gehlert

Photo credits:
All photographs by Tina and Horst Herzig with the exception of: pp. 20/21: bofotolux/iStockphoto.com; pp. 26/27: inter light/iStockphoto.com; pp. 88/89: danako/ iStockphoto.com; pp. 110/111: JurgaR/iStockphoto.com.

ISBN 978-3-8003-4143-6

See our entire catalogue at:
www.verlagshaus.com